RosettaStone®

User's Guide

Printed in the United States of America.

ISBN 978-1-60391-833-6

Rosetta Stone
Harrisonburg, Virginia USA
T (540) 432-6166 • (800) 788-0822 in USA and Canada
F (540) 432-0953
RosettaStone.com

Welcome!

Welcome to Rosetta Stone° — the world's leading language-learning software.

Rosetta Stone teaches language naturally, the same way you learned your first language, by connecting words to objects and events around you. Native speakers and thousands of real-life images help you think in the new language from the very beginning.

You select a course that meets your learning goals.

You'll understand everyday language through our proficiency-based listening and reading activities.

You'll pronounce words correctly after practicing with our proprietary speech recognition and analysis tool.

You'll speak without a script. Contextual Formation™ makes sure you have the confidence and the cues you need to get the words out on the spot.

You'll spell and write accurately, building gradually from letters to words and sentences.

You'll engage in real-life conversations. With our Milestone activities, gain confidence using speech alone to get around and get what you need.

You'll retain what you learn. Our unique Adaptive Recall™ reinforces language so it sticks with you in the real world.

With Rosetta Stone you'll be reading and speaking a language in no time. No translation. No grammar rules. Rosetta Stone is the fastest way to learn a new language.

Enjoy the Rosetta Stone experience.

Table of Contents

The Rosetta Stone Story

In 1799, French soldiers uncovered a large piece of carved basalt. The discovery was significant, for the writing on the stone appeared in two languages and three scripts. The soldiers were stationed in the nearby town of Rosetta (Rashid), Egypt. The carved basalt rock became known as the Rosetta Stone. It was nearly 2000 years old. A group of priests had created the stone in 196 BC to honor Ptolemy V Epiphanes, pharaoh of Egypt.

Decoding Egyptian Hieroglyphs

The Rosetta Stone was the key to unlocking the mystery of ancient Egyptian hieroglyphs. The writing was divided into three sections. Each contained the same message.

At the time of the inscription, Egyptians wrote in three scripts: Egyptian hieroglyphs, demotic Egyptian, and Greek. Each script had a specific use. Religious and other important documents were composed in hieroglyphs, everyday writings used the demotic script, and the rulers spoke and wrote Greek. The writers of the Rosetta Stone ensured that all priests, government officials, and rulers could read the message and appreciate its significance.

Jean-Francois Champollion, a French linguist, took the first steps toward understanding ancient Egyptian culture and language when he deciphered both the ideograms (pictures that represent things or ideas) and phonograms (pictures that represent sounds) engraved on the Rosetta Stone.

Language Learning and Technology

This priceless artifact represents the key to solving a great mystery. Just as the stone unlocked the mysteries of ancient Egypt, our software unlocks understanding of new languages and cultures.

Rosetta Stone® language-learning software was first developed in 1991. Rosetta Stone uses two principles that are the core of our philosophy of language learning: 1) The way we learn language as children — immersion in that language — is the best way to learn a new language at any age. 2) Interactive technology is a powerful tool for replicating and activating that process.

Today, Rosetta Stone is the world's leading language-learning software.

The Rosetta Stone® Method

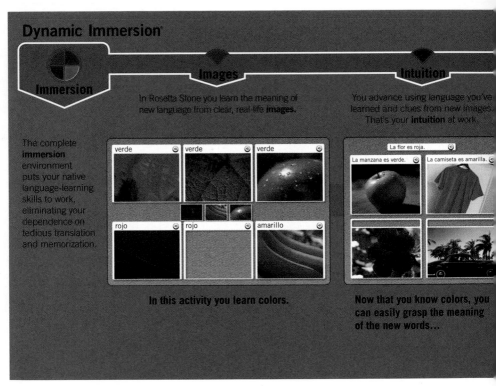

Dynamic Immersion®

Immersion

The complete **immersion** environment puts your native language-learning skills to work, eliminating your dependence on tedious translation and memorization.

Images

In Rosetta Stone you learn the meaning of new language from clear, real-life **images.**

Intuition

You advance using language you've learned and clues from new images. That's your **intuition** at work.

| verde | verde | verde |
| rojo | rojo | amarillo |

In this activity you learn colors.

| La flor es roja. |
| La manzana es verde. | La camiseta es amarilla. |

Now that you know colors, you can easily grasp the meaning of the new words...

Interactivity

Throughout Rosetta Stone, you constantly **interact** with the program to confirm your intuition.

...and then check what you've learned.

Instruction

From beginning to end you build systematically toward your language-learning goals, for the most effective and enjoyable **instruction** anywhere.

And finally, you get the fun of trying your new language in a real-life simulation. Speech recognition shows you exactly how you're doing.

Learning a Language

We made Rosetta Stone® for you to use naturally, at your own pace, drawing on the same power of immersion you used to learn your first language. Absorb the sounds of your new language. Observe the images for meaning. As you spend time working in Rosetta Stone, you learn a language easily.

As you experience Rosetta Stone, you may have questions about how to best use the software. We've provided some guidelines for you to follow.

Trust the Method

Rosetta Stone succeeds in teaching you a new language without translation. We don't want you to think of an idea or concept in your native language to recall a word in your new one.

Instead, our method is natural. We match spoken dialogue and text with photographic images from real life. That's immersion.

On every screen we give you just enough information to move ahead. As you finish each screen, you'll learn a little more. After a while, you'll realize that you are learning the structure and vocabulary of your new language.

Follow the Sequence

As you start the program, we ask you to choose your course based on your learning goals. Select a full range of Activities, or focus on reading, listening, writing or speaking. We customize your course to your needs.

As you complete each Lesson, additional Activities allow you to practice what you learned. You'll use the Lesson content to practice language skills such as reading, listening, writing, or speaking. Each Unit concludes with a Milestone to let you practice key skills learned in the Unit and apply your new language knowledge in a real-life situation.

Give It Your Best Try

- Compare images, and don't worry if you don't know what a word means the first time. You'll have many chances to learn.
- Choose an answer. If you are correct, move ahead. If not, you probably now know the answer and can progress. Either way, you've learned new language without translation.

Work Outside the Software

We find the best learning model is one based on multiple methods and media.

- Use your new vocabulary to post notes on everyday objects in your home or living quarters.
- Find others with whom you can speak or write your new language. Recombine words and phrases you've learned to form new sentences.
- Travel to an area where people speak the language, or read newspapers, magazines, or Web sites in your new language.

Enjoy this software. You'll discover a world where words, sounds, and imagery work together to immerse you in a new language. You'll add to your knowledge with every step, without translation.

Using this Guide

This guide was designed with you in mind. The software is intuitive, but we have also provided support in a format we know you'll find easy to use.

Part of this guide is arranged in a tutorial style. From the beginning, start using your Rosetta Stone software by following simple guides that walk you through the steps to set up your Course and complete a Core Lesson.

Other parts of the guide provide reference material. Use these references if you have questions about screen types, language skills, and screen elements.

The sidebars, or outer columns of this User's Guide, contain directions for completing screens. Yellow bars contain **Tips**, **Need More Info?**, and **How To...** text. You'll find information about the Activities in the center of the pages. Screen shots illustrate the guide.

Use the Help icon at the top of your screen to get help with specific screens. Additional help is available online.

Enjoy your language-learning experience!

Follow Instructions

Learn How to Complete a Related Function

Need More Information?

Practice Speaking

The **Speech** screen may appear with or without text.

1. At the Record prompt, speak into the microphone. The border on the Record icon indicates your level of accuracy.

2. If you pronounce the phrase incorrectly, you will be prompted to repeat the phrase.

3. If you are unable to complete a screen, click the right arrow at the bottom of the screen to advance to the next screen.

How to ...

To disable speech recognition, go to the Toolbar at the top of the screen. Click **Preferences**, then uncheck the box that says **use speech recognition**.

Need More Info?

To set speech precision levels, see *page 47*.

Practice Speaking

Speech screens help you master spoken language

Rosetta Stone uses Speech Recognition technolo patterns. We also use Contextual Formation,™ wh learned. Several types of speech screens offer s

- Practice Speaking
- Produce a Phrase or Sentence
- Speech Analysis

un sándwich

pan

un h

café

Chapter 1

Start Learning with Rosetta Stone*

Follow Your Course

Set Up Your Course

Set Up the Microphone

Complete a Core Lesson

Follow Your Course

Rosetta Stone® is structured to make it simple for you to reach goals, and flexible so you can easily progress through learning a new language.

We create an individualized course for you — a lesson series tailored to your language-learning goals.

Achieving Language-Learning Goals

Each Rosetta Stone level has several Units, each of which focuses on a language topic. Each Unit has four Core Lessons, several Focused Activities and a Milestone. In Core Lessons you learn language using a full range of skills: reading, listening, speaking, and writing exercises. Focused Activities include exercises that concentrate on one of these language skills. Milestones allow you to practice your new language using real-life scenarios.

In your course, we determine the order of the activities based on selections you make the first time you log in to Rosetta Stone. Our recommended course takes you through every language skill in Rosetta Stone with the goal of language proficiency.

Your course includes Core Lessons and a combination of Focused Activities. It may include an emphasis on particular learning skills. For example, you may feel confident with reading and listening to the language and want to focus on pronunciation. Following your course, you'll achieve your language-learning goals.

Click **Start** on the Home screen to follow your course.

Completing a Core Lesson

In the tutorial on the following pages, you first complete the Core Lesson from Unit 1, Lesson 1. You learn to recognize words and phrases. These screens use a combination of written and spoken words with pictures and are designed to use your natural language-learning capacity.

In some screens you see pictures associated with words, and you are prompted to provide a missing piece to the puzzle. Sometimes a native speaker says words or phrases, and you choose a representative picture. At times you may hear the native speaker but not see the text; you select the picture that matches the phrase spoken by the native speaker.

Building on Language Skills

You begin speaking your new language immediately when prompted to repeat after the native speaker. The software uses speech recognition to indicate whether you have pronounced the words and phrases correctly.

Rosetta Stone uses your natural ability to associate words and images by providing prompts and then asking you to continue the "conversation." We call this process Contextual Formation™ because you learn the language well enough to form your own responses in the context of a "real-life" situation.

Start using Rosetta Stone now by following the tutorial that begins on the next page.

Set Up Your Course

Activate a Language:

1. Enter the Activation ID
   that came with your
   Rosetta Stone® software.

2. Click **Activate** to activate
   the product. If you do not
   have Internet access, you
   will be prompted to activate
   by phone.

Create a User:

1. Enter a user name in the
   field provided.

2. Select **Male** or **Female**
   to optimize speech
   recognition.

3. Click **Save changes.**

After installation and before you begin your course, Rosetta Stone
asks you to activate your new language. You will activate each new
language you purchase and install using an ID you received with
your software. If you choose to activate later, you will have access
to limited Rosetta Stone content. Once the language has been
activated, you are ready to create a user. Select **Male** or **Female** to
help Rosetta Stone's speech recognition function correctly process
your voice.

Tip

You can choose **Activate
Later** to get started using the
software. Some Rosetta Stone
content will be available for use.
Some lessons will be locked
until activation.

Build Your Course

Rosetta Stone builds a Course based on your goals. The first time you launch Rosetta Stone, you will see the Select Your Course screen. Select the **Recommended** Course, which incorporates all four language skills — Reading, Writing, Speaking, and Listening — or select from the alternate Courses to focus learning on specific skills or to add letters and sounds. You can always change your Course later through Preferences, located on the Toolbar. After you click **Next**, Rosetta Stone will build your Course. Click anywhere on the screen to continue after each step.

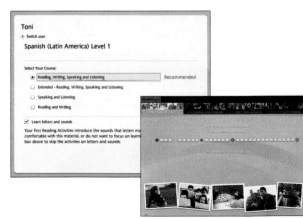

Select Your Course:

1. To choose a Course, click on the desired **Course**.
   Note: Some languages use more than one script. Click the script system you want to learn.
2. Click **Next.**
3. The Home screen appears and Rosetta Stone begins building your Course step by step. Click anywhere on the screen to continue after each step.

Need More Info?

To learn how to change your Course, *see page 60*.

You may also access a Core Lesson in a Unit from the Course View on the Home screen by selecting the Unit and then clicking one of the Core Lesson diamonds on the Course Bar.

Need More Info?

To learn more about the Home screen, *see page 24*.

Start Your Course

An introductory video appears on the Home screen the first time you launch the Course. The Home screen is your information center. From here you click **Start** to enter an activity in your Course. (Once you begin an Activity, this icon will change to say Continue.) The screen also illustrates your progress through the software. You can view your progress on the Course Bar. A check mark appears when you have completed an Activity. You can also change Preferences and get Help from the Toolbar at the top of the screen.

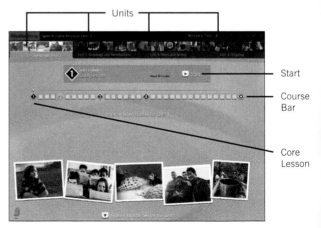

Rosetta Stone® User's Guide

Set Up the Microphone

The advanced speech recognition and analysis tool guides you to more accurate pronunciation. You speak into the microphone, and the software provides feedback to help you adjust your pronunciation to match that of the native speaker.

Use the Microphone Setup screen to allow the speech recognition tool to adjust to the normal tone of your voice. You can also access Audio Settings to set the Speech Precision Level or to specify a different microphone in later sessions.

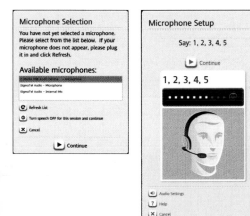

Set Up the Microphone:

1. Select the correct microphone when you see the Microphone Selection screen.
2. Click **Continue**.
3. Click **Continue** when the Microphone Setup screen appears.
4. Speak into the microphone in a normal tone. Say "1, 2, 3, 4, 5".
5. When you get confirmation that the Microphone Setup was successful, click **Continue**.

Need More Info?

To learn more about speech precision levels, *see page 62-63.*

Complete a Core Lesson

Get Started:

1. For most screens in the Lesson, a prompt appears, and you select the image or text that best matches or completes the prompt.

2. If your selection is correct, a green check appears. If incorrect, an orange X appears.

3. After you complete the first screen in the Lesson, the screen pauses then auto advances.

The Core Lesson is the main exercise that teaches you language. The Focused Activities, which we will look at later, concentrate on specific language skills.

In the Core Lesson you learn words and create phrases. From the first Activity you begin to read, listen, and speak in this new language.

This tutorial begins with Unit 1, Lesson 1 to help you learn how Rosetta Stone teaches language. In this first Activity, the Core Lesson, you learn nouns and the proper articles for each noun type. You add verbs to create phrases or short sentences.

This tutorial shows you the types of screens that appear in the Core Lesson and provides instruction for completing each type of screen.

Choose the Image

When you see a phrase and hear the native speaker, you are prompted to choose a matching picture. This screen type reinforces both listening and reading skills. To view the correct answers, click the **Answers** icon located on the lower left corner of the screen.

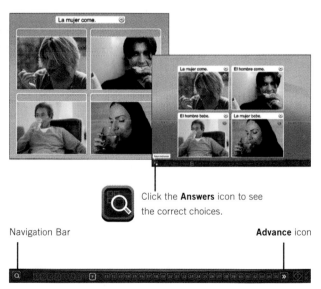

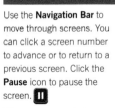

Click the **Answers** icon to see the correct choices.

Navigation Bar

Advance icon

Choose the Image:

1. Listen to the native speaker and read the phrase that appears at the top of the screen.
2. Select the picture that best matches the phrase by clicking anywhere inside the picture.
3. Continue for each new phrase that appears at the top of the screen.

How to...

Use the **Navigation Bar** to move through screens. You can click a screen number to advance or to return to a previous screen. Click the **Pause** icon to pause the screen.

When you are ready to continue, click the **Advance** icon. »

Listen to the Native Speaker

Listen to the Speaker:

On some screens, text is absent; you only hear the native speaker and see images.

1. Listen to the native speaker.

2. Click on the picture to select the image that best matches the phrase you hear.

Some screens do not have text. Listen to the native speaker and choose the picture that matches the phrase you hear. This screen type focuses on listening skills. To hear the native speaker repeat the phrase, click the **Speaker** icon at the top of the screen.

Tip

To hear the native speaker repeat the words, click the **Speaker** icon above the picture.

Practice Your Speech

Some screens offer you the opportunity to practice your
new language. In some cases our native speaker helps
you. Repeat after the speaker. You have several opportunities
to repeat the phrase.

Speaker icon

Practice Your Speech:

1. Read the phrase and listen to the native speaker.

2. Click the **Speaker** icon to hear the native speaker repeat the phrase.

3. Repeat after the native speaker. Speak after you hear the tone.

4. Continue to repeat after the native speaker for each screen in this exercise.

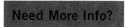

Need More Info?

For more information on the Speech Analysis function, *see page 46*.

Produce a Phrase

Produce a Phrase:

1. Examine the clues in
   the pictures and text to
   determine a correct phrase
   that represents the picture
   without text.

2. Speak into the microphone
   and produce a phrase that
   best represents the picture.
   Use words you learned
   in this lesson.

Some speech screens require you to produce a phrase without the
help of our native speaker. This screen type requires you to use your
intuition and your new language skills to produce a phrase. The new
phrase will consist of words you have already learned.

View Your Score

Your score appears at the end of the Activity. The green check shows the number of prompts you answered correctly. The orange X shows the number of incorrect answers. You can also see the number of screens you skipped or chose not to answer. The score screen also allows you the opportunity to continue to the next Activity or to return to the home screen.

View Your Score:

Your score will appear at the end of the Activity.

1. Note that the score screen shows correct, incorrect, and skipped answers.

2. You have several options. The following are the most common:
   - Continue to the next Activity
   - Return Home

Tip

You can view your score at any time, from any screen, by mousing over the **Score** icon at the bottom right of the screen.

Chapter 2

Using Rosetta Stone® Tools

Explore the Home Screen

The Home screen is your information center. You can watch an introductory video, change Preferences and get Help. The Home screen has two views: the Course View and the Explore View. Use the Course View to follow your selected course. The Explore View allows you to see and access all Activities.

The Course View

The Course View is your gateway to your selected Rosetta Stone® Course. From here you click **Start** to enter your Course, or click **Continue** if you are returning to your Course. This screen displays progress through your Course, established when you selected the Course using the Course Setup screen.

Use the Bold Words to Help You Identify the Parts of the Course View Home Screen:

- Each Level has four **Units**. Select a Unit to show its Lessons.

- To select a Lesson, click a **diamond** icon on the **Course Bar** or select **Start** or **Continue**.

- Each Unit has four **Lessons** and one **Milestone** that appear in full color when the Unit is selected.

- Each **Lesson** has a series of Activities, represented by the square icons in the row. A check mark indicates you have completed the **Activity**.

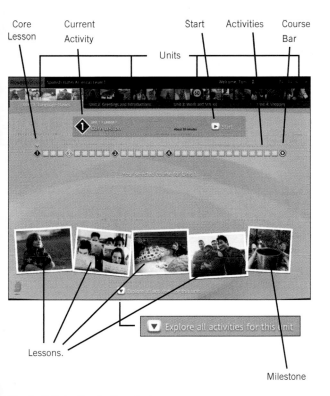

Core Lesson   Current Activity   Start   Activities   Course Bar

Units

Lessons.

Explore all activities for this unit

Milestone

- The **Milestone** occurs at the end of each Unit. This series of exercises tests your skills.

- Move the mouse over a square **Activity** icon on the **Course Bar** to display that **Activity**.

- A **Core Lesson** uses a variety of skill sets to reinforce learning. A **Focused Activity** focuses on a particular skill set, such as Pronunciation.

- To view all Activities in the Unit, click **Explore all activities for this unit**.

The Explore View

The Explore View shows all Activities in a Unit. Each Unit contains four Lessons. Each Lesson includes a Core Lesson, Focused Activities, and a Review. The Core Lesson includes a variety of exercises designed to introduce you to new content. The Focused Activities allow you to practice specific language skills.

Use the Bold Words to Help You Identify the Parts of the Explore Screen:

- The **Activity Banners** below each Lesson photo contain a **Core Lesson, Focused Activities,** and a **Review**.

- Each Lesson has a variety of Activities. The **Core Lesson** has several exercise types. The **Focused Activities** allow you to practice specific language skills.

- A highlighted **Activity** is included in your selected Course.

- If the Activity is not highlighted, that Activity is not included in your Course, although you may click on these Activities to access them.

- Click **Return to your Course** to return to the Course View.

Return to your Course   Activity Banner

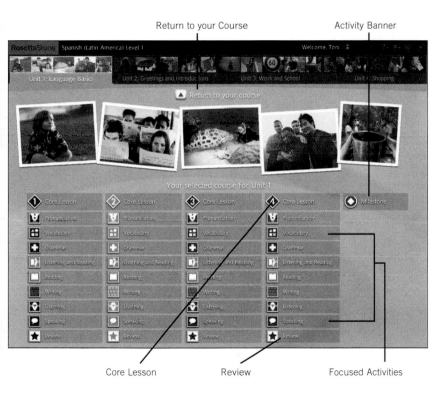

Core Lesson   Review   Focused Activities

The Toolbar

Your personalized Toolbar displays your Course language and level and offers Preferences and a Help screen. From the Toolbar you can access a video that introduces you to Rosetta Stone. You can also set or change Preferences. You can access these tools anytime the Toolbar appears at the top of the screen, or return to the Home screen to access the Toolbar.

Use the Bold Words to Help You Identify Icons on the Toolbar:

- The Toolbar displays the **Language and Level** you are studying. If you have more than one Language Level installed, an arrow will indicate that other languages are available for study. Click the arrow to view other languages.

- Select the **Preferences** pull-down menu to change settings for display and speech or to watch the introductory video.

- Select the **Help** pull-down menu to learn more about the current screen or other functions in Rosetta Stone.

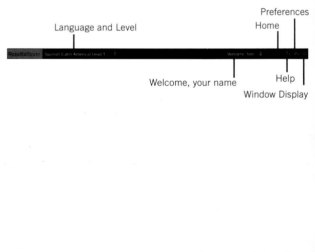

Language and Level

Preferences

Home

Welcome, your name

Help

Window Display

- From the **Home** screen, click the **User** icon to log in as a new user. If you are in a Lesson, click on the **Home** icon to return to the **Home** screen.

- Click the **Window** icon to toggle between a fullscreen display and a resizable window display.

- Click **Sign Out** to exit Rosetta Stone from fullscreen display.

Change User   Preferences   Help

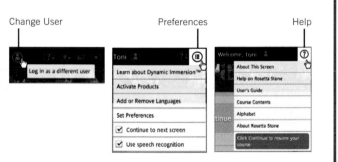

**Use the Bold Words to Help
You Identify Icons on the Unit
Bar and Course Bar:**

- The **Unit Bar** represents
  your Course by showing
  all four Units. Each Unit
  is represented by a group
  of photos at the top of
  the screen.

- Each Unit has four **Lessons**
  and a **Milestone**.

- Completed Activities are
  marked on the **Course Bar**.

- The **Activity Name** appears
  in the Course Bar as you
  select an Activity.

- Click an **Activity** icon to
  launch the Activity.

The Unit Bar and Course Bar

Enter Units through the Unit Bar. Click **Start** to begin an Activity
or click **Continue** and the program will take you to where you were
last working. Use the Course Bar to navigate to Activities and to
follow your progress.

Unit Bar

Course Bar

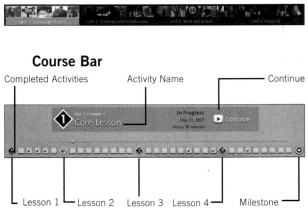

Rosetta Stone® User's Guide

Lessons and Milestone

- Each picture at the bottom of the screen represents a **Lesson**.

- Each Lesson has several Activities. The Activity icons are color-coded to the corresponding photo.

- Select **Start** to begin a new Activity or **Continue** to return to an Activity. Rosetta Stone will take you to the Activity on which you were last working.

Focused Activities

Focused Activities allow you to concentrate on specific language skills or a combination of skills. They may include a few specialized screen types designed to emphasize these skills.

Your Course contains a selection of the following Activities:

- Core Lesson
- Pronunciation
- Vocabulary
- Grammar

- Listening and Reading
- Reading
- Writing
- Listening

- Speaking
- Review

In Explore View, Activities in the Lesson color are included in your Course. Grayed Activities are not included in your Course. You can select any Activity from Explore View.

The **Core Lesson** is the main Activity that teaches language. It includes a variety of exercises designed to introduce you to new language content.

The **Pronunciation** Activity focuses on refining your pronunciation by breaking down the words and giving you detailed visual feedback to compare your speech to that of the native speaker.

Vocabulary is reinforced through a combination of images, reading, and listening exercises to help you practice your new words.

The **Grammar** Activity helps you focus on the grammatical structures of the language you have learned.

Rosetta Stone builds on **Listening and Reading** skills to reinforce the connection between spoken and written text.

The **Reading** Activity introduces sounds and letters from your new language and builds your reading ability as you learn.

The **Writing** Activity guides you into recognizing the alphabet and learning to spell words in the language you are learning.

The **Listening** Activity provides added training in listening comprehension.

The **Speaking** Activity gives you plenty of speech practice, so you're confident speaking right away.

The **Review** brings back content you've mastered in previous Activities for reinforcement.

Milestones

A Milestone appears at the end of each Unit. A Milestone presents a real-life scenario and allows you to practice what you've learned by participating in the conversation. Use what you learned in the Unit and the context of the scenario to form questions and answers.

Follow the scenario by watching the pictures slide across your screen. These pictures tell a story. The people in the scenario speak and sometimes ask you questions. Respond to the prompts in the conversation with speech that fits the context, and form questions for others to answer.

Participate in a Conversation:

1. Follow the scenario by watching the pictures slide across your screen.
2. When the conversation begins, use the verbal and visual prompts to answer the questions.
3. As the conversation continues, follow the prompts and form questions or answers that fit the context.

Review and Adaptive Recall™ Activities

Rosetta Stone has several processes to help you successfully learn your new language. We prompt you to review and recall earlier language skills as you learn new ones. We start this process when we build your Course. As you progress to new Lessons, Rosetta Stone includes Activities from earlier Lessons with new ones to reinforce language skills. Rosetta Stone also provides periodic reviews.

Building Your Course

Rosetta Stone builds your Course to help you learn efficiently. We include Reviews to help you master your skills as you focus on new material.

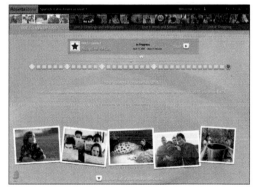

Review

Each Lesson includes a Review that evaluates you on the material you have learned to that point.

Adaptive Recall

Adaptive Recall schedules review material to reappear at an optimal time to help move language to your long-term memory.

As you master the language, Adaptive Recall appears at longer intervals.

The Navigation Bar is disabled during Review and Adaptive Recall Activities.

Script Systems

Some languages use more than one script for their writing systems. Depending on the language you are learning, you may see a prompt to choose a script when you select your course. Within an Activity, script buttons at the bottom of the screen make it easy to switch between scripts.

Change the script system you are learning:

Click the script buttons at the bottom of the Activity screen.

Note: Some script options contain small superscript characters to assist your reading and pronunciation. Click the magnifying glass to enlarge the superscript charcters.

Need More Info?

To learn more about the scripts for the language you are learning, see the Help menu option for learning your language.

Chapter 3

Completing Rosetta Stone® Screens

Learn to Use the Screens

Rosetta Stone® uses a variety of screen types to immerse you in the language. We have provided this quick reference to show you some examples of how you will respond to screens. Instructions for completing each are on the following pages.

Make a Selection or Speak

- **Choose Image:** choose the image that matches the spoken phrase.

- **Choose Prompt:** choose the prompt that matches the image.

- **Speech Practice:** speak into the microphone to supply the correct phrase.

- **Speech Production:** speak into the microphone to form a new phrase using word and image clues.

Choose Image

Choose Prompt

Speech Practice

Speech Production

Pronounce Syllables

Use a Microphone or Keyboard

- **Pronounce Syllables:** speak into the microphone to repeat the missing syllable.

Speech Analysis

Multiple Choice

- **Speech Analysis:** record your voice and repeat after the native speaker.

- **Multiple Choice:** choose a word or phrase to complete the phrase or sentence.

Writing and Typing

- **Writing and Typing:** type the phrase using your keyboard, or use your mouse to click the on-screen keyboard.

Choose an Image

Choose an Image

Click on the image that best matches the prompt.

In this screen type, you supply the missing piece by selecting an image to match the prompt. This screen teaches you language by association of words and meaning derived from images. Listen to the native speaker say the prompt. You may or may not see text at the top of the screen. Click on the image that best matches the prompt.

Choose a Prompt

The Choose a Prompt screen also teaches you language by associating words with meaning derived through images. This screen uses text or pictures as prompts at the top of the screen to be matched with pictures or text boxes below. In this screen type the missing piece may be text or an image.

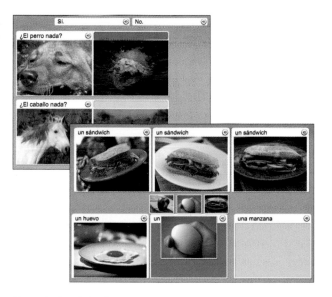

Choose the Phrase

1. Several text prompts appear above a picture. The native speaker will read one of the phrases.
2. Click on the phrase that matches the picture.

Choose the Picture

1. Several picture prompts appear above text boxes.
2. Click the picture that best matches the highlighted text box.

If you choose the correct answer, you will move to the next task. If you choose incorrectly, you will be prompted to choose another.

Practice Speaking

Speech screens help you master spoken language and develop conversation skills. Your voice provides the missing piece.

Rosetta Stone® uses Speech Recognition technology and a unique method of speech analysis to evaluate your speech patterns. We also use Contextual Formation,™ which asks you to produce new phrases using the language you have learned. Several types of speech screens offer several ways for you to master speech in your new language:

- Practice Speaking
- Produce a Phrase or Sentence
- Speech Analysis

Practice Speaking

The **Speech** screen may appear with or without text.

1. At the Record prompt, speak into the microphone. The border on the Record icon indicates your level of accuracy.

2. If you pronounce the phrase incorrectly, you will be prompted to repeat the phrase.

3. If you are unable to complete a screen, click the right arrow at the bottom of the screen to advance to the next screen.

How to ...

To disable speech recognition, go to the Toolbar at the top of the screen. Click **Preferences**, then uncheck the box that says **use speech recognition**.

Produce a New Phrase or Sentence

Our Contextual Formation learning method allows you to produce new phrases and sentences on your own. We prompt you carefully, using words and pictures. You produce a new word or phrase that fits the context. This prepares you for the challenge of real-life conversation.

Produce a New Phrase

1. Study the images.
2. Say a new phrase or sentence into the microphone, using the context of the images and other text on the screen.

Need More Info?

To set speech precision levels, *see page 62*.

Pronounce Syllables

Pronounce the Word:

1. Listen to the native speaker say the word.

2. Repeat each syllable after the speaker.

3. Put the syllables together to say the word.

The Pronunciation screen teaches language syllable by syllable. This screen type focuses on correct pronunciation by breaking down words into syllables. Repeat each syllable after the native speaker. Put the syllables together to pronounce the word correctly.

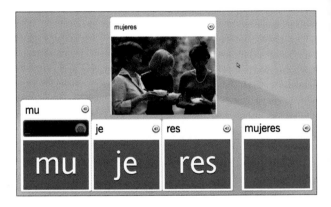

Select from Multiple Choices

The Multiple Choice screens provide training on the structure of the language you are learning. For example, you may connect articles to nouns, form singular and plural words, or determine masculine and feminine forms.

From the options, click on the one that correctly completes the phrase or sentence.

Choose the Correct Option:

1. Read the phrase or sentence with the missing word.

2. From the options presented, click to select the answer that correctly completes the phrase or sentence.

3. If you select the incorrect answer, you will be prompted to choose another. If you select the correct answer, your choice will appear in the blank and you will move to the next task.

Use Speech Analysis

Rosetta Stone® uses Speech Analysis to help you evaluate your speech patterns as you repeat after the native speaker. Graphs on the Speech Analysis screen show speech patterns.

On any speech screen, click the **Speech Analysis** icon to open a new screen. The icon is gray, but becomes highlighted as you scroll your mouse over it. On other screen types this icon is available, but you must click the **Answers** icon to access the Speech Analysis icon.

On speech screens, the native speaker's voice plays at a slow speed and a Record prompt appears. Mimic the speaker's voice to see a graph of your voice and use the **Record** icon to record again. Click the appropriate **Speaker** icon to review a recording.

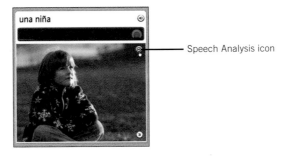

Speech Analysis icon

How To ...

To use the Speech Analysis function, click the **Speech Analysis** icon on any speech screen. On other types of screens, use the **Answers** icon to access the Speech Analysis icon.

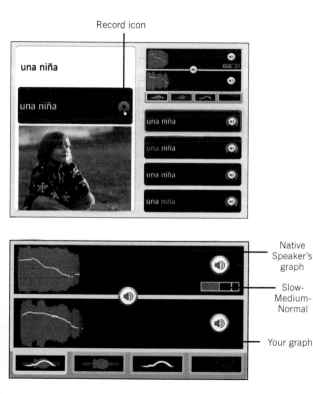

Record icon

Compare Your Speech to the Native Speaker's Speech:

1. Click the **Speech Analysis** icon.

2. Listen to the native speaker and watch the voice graph.

3. At the **Record** prompt, speak into the microphone. Mimic the native speaker's voice; use the graph as a guide.

4. If you are not satisfied with your pronunciation, try again. Click the Record icon and speak into the microphone. The arc on the Record icon indicates your level of accuracy.

Tip

Speech defaults to slow speed.
Move the speech control to change the speed of the native speaker's voice.

Native Speaker's graph

Slow-Medium-Normal

Your graph

Evaluate Speech Using Graphs

Use the Graphs to Refine Your Speech Patterns:

1. Click the **Speaker** icon on your recording history to listen to your recording and compare the graph to the native speaker's graph.

2. Click the **Graph** icons to review speech patterns in one of four ways.

The graphs on the speech analysis screen help you evaluate and improve your speech patterns by giving you a visual comparison of your speech with the native speaker's speech. Click a tab to display a speech graph.

Emphasis and Pitch displays the combination of the strength of your speech and the high to low pitch change.

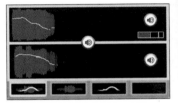

Emphasis displays the strength of your speech to compare the relative stress.

Pitch displays your voice's high to low change in pitch.

Spectrogram displays the strength of voice frequencies over time, also known as a Voiceprint.

Practice Writing

Rosetta Stone® helps you learn how to write in the language you're studying. One of the ways you learn to write words and phrases is by typing the words and phrases as you read and hear them.

The purpose of the Writing screen is to teach you how to spell words in the language you're learning. It also familiarizes you with the alphabet for the language. The typing exercise is only one of several screen types used to reinforce writing skills.

In this typing exercise, use the clues in other photos to help you determine the missing piece; then type the correct word or phrase. In some screens the text clues will aid you. Other screens are more challenging; you'll only hear the native speaker say the words or phrases, and you must type what you hear.

Use your keyboard to type the letters, or use your mouse to click the correct letters using the on-screen keyboard.

see illustrations on next page

Type a Phrase:

1. Identify the photo with the highlighted empty space.
2. Read or listen to the clues on the screen, and type the missing phrase in the empty space above the photo.
3. Click **Enter** on the keyboard.

Incorrect Answers:

The incorrect letter will be highlighted. Correct the mistake to move to the next task. If you type more than one incorrect letter, each incorrect letter will be highlighted until you correct it.

Practice Writing, continued

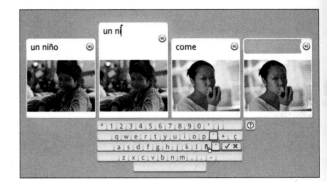

How To ...

- Use your keyboard to type text, or use your mouse to click the letters using the on-screen keyboard.
- Click a special character key to select additional characters with accent or diacritic marks.
- Click **Enter** to check your score.

Need More Info?

To learn more about changing the typing precision level and the keyboard layout, *see page 58*.

Special character keys

Chapter 4

Changing User Options

Log In as a Different/New User

Log In:

1. From the Home screen, click on the **Change User** icon in the Toolbar to log in as a different user.

2. To create a new user, click **Add a user** and enter a user name in the box.

3. Select **Male** or **Female** to help Rosetta Stone recognize your voice.

4. Click **Save changes**.

5. To select a user, click on the **User Name** and click **Start.**

Change User

Create a user:

Toni

Rosetta Stone Speech Recognition performs best when it knows your voice type:

● Female   ○ Male

✓ Save changes

Select Your Course

1. Keep **Recommended** selected.

2. Or, select one of three alternate Courses based on your goals.

3. Click the box **Learn letters and sounds** if you wish to learn the alphabet and phonics for the language studied.

Note: Some languages use more than one script. Click the script system you want to learn.

4. Click **Next**.

Need More Info?

To change your Course later, see **Change Your Course** on *page 60*.

Preferences

Watch the Introductory Video:

1. Click the **Preferences** icon located on the Toolbar.

2. Click **Learn about Dynamic Immersion:** The video begins automatically.

3. To pause, click the **Pause** icon.

4. To close the video and return to the Home screen, click the red **X** in the upper right-hand corner of the video.

The first time you open Rosetta Stone, a video introduces you to Dynamic Immersion, our language-learning method. Access this video at any time from the Preferences menu, located on the Toolbar. Use Preferences to activate new products, add or remove languages, or change a variety of settings. Check the box labeled **Continue to next screen** if you want Activity screens to advance automatically. Check **Use speech recognition** if you want to practice speaking.

Activate Products

Activate your new language using the Activation ID you received when you purchased Rosetta Stone.

Or, you may choose **Activate Later** to access limited Rosetta Stone content. You can still activate the entire product at any time.

Product Activation

Activate your Rosetta Stone language product to access all the lessons. You have access to limited lessons until you activate. Activating by Internet is fastest and easiest. Enter the Activation ID that came with your product (only one ID needed for a multi-level set). Click Activate. If you do not have an Internet connection, you will be prompted to activate by phone.

Unactivated Products	Activated Products

Spanish (Latin America) Level 1

[ ] - [ ] - [ ] - [ ] - [ ]

▶ Activate   » Activate Later

Activate Products

1. Click the **Preferences** icon located on the Toolbar.

2. Click **Activate Products** in the pull-down menu.

3. Enter the Activation ID that came with your software.

4. Click **Activate** to connect to the Internet and activate the product. If you do not have Internet access, activate by phone.

5. Click **Activate Later** to postpone activation and work with limited Rosetta Stone content.

Add or Remove Languages

Add a Language Level:

1. Click the **Preferences** icon located on the Toolbar.

2. Click **Add or Remove Languages.**

3. Click **Add a Language Level.**

4. Follow the prompt to insert the Language Level CD and select the language.

5. Click **Install selected language.** This process may take time.

6. Once the installation is complete, click **Continue launching application.**

Use the **Add or Remove Languages** screen to install a new language or remove a Language Level. Removing a language may be useful when you want to create room on your computer to install a new language. You may reinstall the language again later.

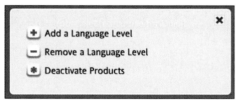

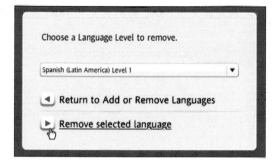

Choose a Language Level to remove.

Spanish (Latin America) Level 1 ▼

◄ Return to Add or Remove Languages

► Remove selected language

Deactivate Products

The Deactivate Products option is for special purposes, such as moving your Rosetta Stone® software from one computer to another. Deactivation is permanent. A product consists of one or more Language Levels that you purchased as a set. You must contact Rosetta Stone Customer Support to complete the deactivation process.

WARNING! Once a Language Level has been deactivated, it cannot be reinstalled. You should only proceed with this option with the advice of Rosetta Stone Customer Support.

Remove Language Level:

1. Click the **Preferences** icon located on the Toolbar.

2. Click **Add or Remove Languages.**

3. Click **Remove a Language Level.**

4. Select the Language Level to be removed.

5. Click **Remove selected language** and **Yes, continue uninstallation.**

6. Click **Continue launching application.**

Need More Info?

For assistance with deactivating a language, contact Rosetta Stone Customer Support. See your *Quick Start Guide* for contact information, or go to RosettaStone.com and click **Support**.

Course Settings

Go To Course Settings:

1. Click the **Preferences** icon located on the Toolbar.

2. Click **Set Preferences** from the pull-down menu.

3. Select the **Course Settings** tab.

Use Course Settings under the Preferences menu to change the precision level of your typing exercises. If you check the boxes, you are required to type using case sensitivity, accurate punctuation, and correct diacritic marks. You can access settings for your selected Course. Depending on your language, you may also be able to change the layout of your keyboard.

Tip

Uncheck all boxes for easiest typing mode.

Set Typing Preferences

Keyboard layout Spanish

Choose Typing Preferences:

1. Click to check the box next to each option to choose that option. By checking any of these options, you are increasing the difficulty level of typing exercises.

2. Use the pull-down menu next to **Keyboard layout** and choose an option. This option refers to the way the keys are arranged on the keyboard. It varies among languages.

3. Click **Apply Changes** to keep new settings, or **Cancel Changes** to return to original settings.

Change Your Course

Go To Course Settings:

1. Click the **Preferences** icon located on the Toolbar.

2. Click **Set Preferences** from the pull-down menu.

3. Select the **Course Settings** tab.

Change Your Course

1. Click **Change your course settings.**

2. Choose a Course that applies to your language-learning needs.

3. Click **Apply Changes** to keep new settings, or **Cancel Changes** to return to original settings.

The Course you selected when you first installed Rosetta Stone® is displayed. You may select a different Course, which will add some Activities and remove others. Complete the new Activities to update your score. Short Courses such as Speaking and Listening, as well as Reading and Writing are more focused on the named language skills. You may add Learn Letters and Sounds to the selected Course, with the exception of Speaking and Listening. Some languages use more than one script. Click the script system you want to learn.

Select Your Course:

- ● Reading, Writing, Speaking and Listening — Recommended
- ○ Extended - Reading, Writing, Speaking and Listening
- ○ Speaking and Listening
- ○ Reading and Writing

☑ Learn letters and sounds

Your first Reading Activities introduce the sounds that letters make. If you're already comfortable with this material, or do not want to focus on learning the letters, uncheck the box above to skip the activities on letters and sounds.

✗ Cancel Changes   **✓ Apply Changes**

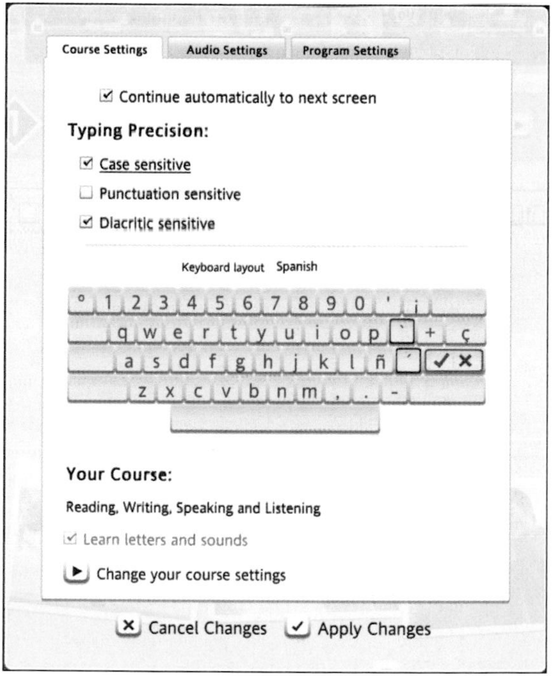

Course Settings | **Audio Settings** | **Program Settings**

☑ Continue automatically to next screen

Typing Precision:

☑ Case sensitive

☐ Punctuation sensitive

☑ Diacritic sensitive

Keyboard layout Spanish

Your Course:

Reading, Writing, Speaking and Listening

☑ Learn letters and sounds

▶ Change your course settings

☒ Cancel Changes   ✓ Apply Changes

Tip

Changing your Course Settings adds some Activities to your course and removes others. New Activities appear in your Course Bar. We recommend you change your Course Setup only if your language-learning goals have changed.

Need More Info?

To find out more about how Rosetta Stone builds your Course, *see page 13*.

Go To Audio Settings:

1. Click the **Preferences** icon located on the Toolbar.
2. Click **Set Preferences** from the pull-down menu.
3. Select the **Audio Settings** tab.

Change Microphones:

1. Connect your microphone to your computer.
2. Click **Refresh List**.
3. Select the correct microphone from the list of available microphones.
4. Click **Microphone Setup** and follow the prompts.
5. Click **Apply Changes**.

Audio Settings

Any setting related to audio devices, Speech Recognition, or other sound settings can be adjusted on the Audio Settings tab.

Change Device Settings

Use the Device Settings to view and select from available microphone Setup to set up your microphone. You can also adjust Speaker Volume. **Note**: For more about Microphone Setup, see page 15.

Change Speech Settings

Use the Speech Recognition Settings to turn speech recognition on to practice speaking your new language. Use this screen to change the precision level of your speech practice. Choose your Voice Type to help Rosetta Stone speech recognition adjust to your voice.

Answer Sounds Settings

You can choose to disable sounds that indicate correct and incorrect answers.

Rosetta Stone® User's Guide

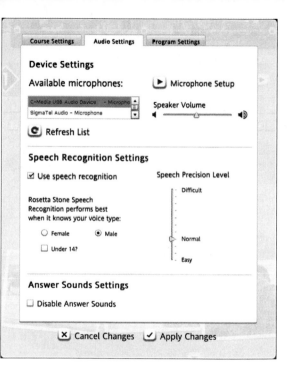

Set Speech Precision Level:

1. Use the slider to select a **Speech Precision Level** to set the software's response to the accuracy of your pronunciation.

2. Select Voice Type: **Male** or **Female**. Check **Under 14?** if you are younger than 14 years old.

3. Click **Apply Changes** to keep new settings, or **Cancel Changes** to return to original settings.

Program Settings

Go To Program Settings:

1. Click the **Preferences** icon located on the Toolbar.

2. Click **Set Preferences** from the pull-down menu.

3. Select the **Program Settings** tab.

Set Interface:

1. Select the language in which you wish your screen information to appear.

2. Click **Apply Changes** to keep new settings, or **Cancel Changes** to return to origional settings.

With the Program Settings tab under the Preferences menu, located on the Toolbar, you can change the language you see in the Rosetta Stone interface. **Note**: This will change the language of screen instructions and menus only. Language study will not change. You can can also check for product updates if your computer is connected to the Internet.

Course Settings	Audio Settings	Program Settings

Rosetta Stone Interface Language:

English ▼

Application Update Settings

▶ Check for Updates
☑ Automatically check for updates

✕ Cancel Changes   ✓ Apply Changes

English ▼

| English |
| Español |
| Deutsch |
| Français |
| Italiano |
| 한국어 |
| 汉语 |
| 日本語 |

Using Help

How can we help you? At Rosetta Stone, we're committed to helping you learn a new language successfully. We want the learning experience to be enjoyable.

One resource we have provided is a Help system within the software. Any time you don't understand something on a screen, click the **Help** icon in the upper right corner of the screen.

We've provided a number of ways for you to learn more about using the software and about the language you are studying.

Find more Rosetta Stone resources on our Web site. Go to RosettaStone.com and click the **Support** link for contact information and helpful information.

Thank you for using Rosetta Stone.

Check for Product Updates:

1. If your Rosetta Stone application does not automatically check for updates, click **Check for Updates**.

2. To have Rosetta Stone automatically check for updates, check **Automatically check for updates**.

3. Click **Apply Changes** to keep new settings, or **Cancel Settings** to return to original settings.

Using the Help Menu:

- View the alphabet for the language.

- Download a PDF of this User's Guide.

- Get instructions for completing the current screen.

Index

Index cont.